STARS OF PRO WRESTLING

★ ★ ★ ★ ★ ★ ★ ★

KURT ANGLE

BY JASON D. NEMETH

Consultant:
Mike Johnson, Writer
PWInsider.com

CAPSTONE PRESS
a capstone imprint

Library of Congress Cataloging-in-Publication Data
Nemeth, Jason D.
    Kurt Angle / by Jason Nemeth.
    p. cm. — (Edge books. stars of pro wrestling)
    Includes bibliographical references and index.
    Summary: "Describes the life and career of pro wrestler Kurt
Angle" — Provided by publisher.
    ISBN 978-1-4296-3945-3 (library binding)
    1. Angle, Kurt — Juvenile literature. 2. Wrestlers — United
States — Biography — Juvenile literature. I. Title.
GV1196.A55N46 2010
796.812092 — dc22   2009027264

Editorial Credits
Kathryn Clay, editor; Kyle Grenz, designer; Jo Miller, media researcher;
    Laura Manthe, production specialist

Photo Credits
AP Images/Michel Lipchitz, 15; DefenseLink/Journalist 1st Class Kristin
Fitzsimmons, cover; Getty Images Inc./Jed Jacobsohn, 17; Getty Images
Inc./Sports Illustrated/George Tiedemann, 10; Globe Photos/John Barrett,
19; Globe Photos/Milan Ryba, 26; Newscom, 21; Newscom/AFP-IOPP/
Georges Gobet, 16; Newscom/Philadelphia Inquirer/MCT/Charles Fox, 29;
Newscom/Scripps Howard News Service/Evan Eile, 18; Newscom/WENN/
David Mepham, 5; Newscom/WENN/Jordan X/Alison Bailey, 6; Shutterstock/
Ken Cave, 13; Wikimedia/Creative Commons/Techarrow, 25; Wikimedia/
Robertlbeukema, 22; Zuma Press/Jason Moore, 9

Design Elements
Shutterstock/amlet; Henning Janos; J. Danny; kzww

TABLE OF CONTENTS

ONE TOUGH MATCH

As Kurt Angle entered the arena at Genesis 2006, a shower of sparks erupted. Draped in the American flag, he jogged down the ramp to the six-sided ring. It was November 19, 2006, and this was Kurt's first major match in Total Nonstop Action (TNA) Wrestling. The 280-pound (127-kilogram) Samoa Joe was already waiting on the mat. Samoa Joe had gone more than 17 months without losing a match. Would Kurt be able to break Samoa Joe's streak?

The match was supercharged from the start. Kurt and Joe locked up. Then Kurt used his Olympic wrestling skills to put Samoa Joe in an *ankle lock*. But Joe kicked out. He beat Kurt back with kicks, punches, and a headbutt.

Kurt *clotheslined* Samoa Joe over the top rope. From outside the ring, Samoa Joe pulled Kurt out by the legs and swung him into the wall. Then Samoa Joe threw him back into the ring and tried for the pin.

Kurt uses the ankle lock to defeat opponents such as Undertaker.

WRESTLING MOVE

ankle lock — the wrestler grabs one of his opponent's legs and twists the ankle

clothesline — a wrestler runs toward the opponent with his arm outstretched and smashes his arm into the opponent's neck

Samoa Joe joined TNA Wrestling in 2005.

THINGS GET UGLY

But Kurt wasn't giving up without a fight. He came back and hit Joe with a series of *European uppercuts*. Then he threw Samoa Joe into a corner and charged him. Samoa Joe moved out of Kurt's way. Kurt smacked his shoulder into a post before falling out of the ring. As Kurt stood up again, Joe charged from the opposite side of the ring. He dove through the ropes to smash Kurt with an elbow. Then Joe grabbed Kurt and slammed his face into the steel steps.

When Kurt finally crawled back into the ring, his head was cut open. Blood was pouring onto the mat. Joe headbutted Kurt right on his cut. Kurt tried to fight back, but he had blood in his eyes. Joe slammed him to the mat.

Maybe Kurt had started a fight with the wrong man.

WRESTLING MOVE

European uppercut — a wrestler swings his forearm up and into his opponent's chin

Chapter 2

UNSTOPPABLE

Kurt Angle was born near Pittsburgh, Pennsylvania, on December 9, 1968. He is the youngest of six children. His older brothers made Kurt wrestle his brother Eric every day. The older brothers also put gloves on Kurt and Eric and made them box each other.

Kurt's father and brothers were all athletic. They expected Kurt to be athletic too. Kurt liked team sports and did well in them. Kurt began wrestling when he was 8 years old. In his first season, he won only two of his 16 matches. He hated to lose, but losing just made him try harder.

HIGH SCHOOL WRESTLING

At Mt. Lebanon High School, Kurt joined the football team and the wrestling team. During his freshman year, he was undefeated in wrestling.

Kurt attended the 2007 CMA festival in Nashville.

In 1992, Kurt (right) wrestled in the NCAA Championship.

WRESTLING FACT

In 10 years of amateur wrestling, Kurt made more than 40 international trips for matches.

Kurt won the Pennsylvania State Wrestling Championship during his senior year of high school. Some college wrestling coaches watched him win. They were hoping to **recruit** Kurt for their teams. Kurt thought about attending the University of Pittsburgh. But he changed his mind after watching a wrestling match at Clarion University. Clarion is a small school just a few hours northeast of Pittsburgh. Though the gym is small, it is often packed full of fans during wrestling matches. Kurt knew Clarion was the right fit for him.

Kurt continued to win matches while at Clarion. He won the NCAA Division I Championship during his sophomore and senior years. He took second place during his junior year.

recruit — to get a person to join

ALMOST GIVING UP

Kurt's next step was to try out for the 1992 Olympic team. Olympic wrestling has different rules than college wrestling. It was hard for Kurt to make the switch, and he didn't make the team.

The next few years were frustrating for Kurt. He kept wrestling but lost many of his matches. Kurt wasn't used to losing, and he thought about quitting wrestling.

In 1994, he tried out for the Pittsburgh Steelers football team. Even though he had a good tryout, it wasn't good enough to make the team. After that, Kurt returned to wrestling. But he knew he would have to change his style to win.

Kurt grew up in the city of Pittsburgh.

A Big Loss

Kurt's father was a crane operator. He helped build many of Pittsburgh's downtown buildings. When Kurt was 16, his father was injured in an accident at work and died two days later. Kurt says that his father's death inspired him to become an Olympic champion.

Chapter 3

GOLD MEDALIST

Changing his style meant training for **endurance** rather than strength. Kurt knew he could win if he outlasted his opponents. He put together a tough daily training routine. The routine included exercises such as running up steep hills while carrying a friend on his back. He also lifted weights and practiced his wrestling moves against Olympic medal winners. Kurt's training helped him win a World Championship in 1995. He also won a chance to compete in the 1996 Olympics in Atlanta, Georgia.

endurance — the ability to keep doing an activity for long periods of time

Kurt worked hard to win an Olympic gold medal.

THE OLYMPICS

After winning four matches, Kurt advanced to the Olympic Finals. His last match was against Iranian Abbas Jadidi, who was a talented wrestler. Kurt knew he could win by tiring out Jadidi. After the standard five-minute match, the wrestlers went into a three-minute overtime. They were tied 1-1 at the end of overtime.

The decision came down to the three referees. They would decide who would win the gold medal. Jadidi seemed confident he had won.

Finally, a referee took their arms. Jadidi put his arm in the air. Kurt thought he'd lost. But the referee pushed Jadidi's arm down and raised Kurt's instead. Kurt had won the gold medal!

Abbas Jadidi (right) won a silver medal at the 1996 Olympics.

A Pain in the Neck

Three months before the 1996 Olympic trials, Kurt broke his neck. He had two broken vertebrae and two disks poking into his spinal cord. Three doctors told Kurt that he could not keep wrestling. But Kurt refused to give up. He found a fourth doctor who would help him.

Before every match, the doctor gave Kurt 12 shots into his neck to numb the pain. It was very dangerous, but Kurt was determined to wrestle in the Olympics. After winning, he told people he won a gold medal with a broken neck.

WRESTLING FACT

Kurt worked briefly for a TV station in Pittsburgh. He was a sportscaster, and his show was called "The Angle on Sports."

Kurt worked as a motivational speaker after winning an Olympic gold medal.

Kurt received a lot of media attention after winning the gold medal. He was interviewed on TV and asked to sponsor products. Kurt also gave motivational speeches. He always told people that if they worked hard they could achieve their dreams just like he did. He finished these talks by telling his audience "It's True! It's True!"

THE WWE

Kurt's Olympic success led to an offer to join the World Wrestling Federation (WWF), which is now called World Wrestling Entertainment (WWE). Kurt turned down the offer. He didn't think pro wrestling required true wrestling skills. But a few years later, he started to rethink his decision.

In 1999, Kurt tried out for the WWF. Unlike amateur wrestling, professional wrestling requires more than athletic skill. It also requires wrestlers to put on a good show for the audience.

Kurt proved to be a good entertainer. He got a WWF contract on his second day. On his fourth day, he was put in a match against Christian.

amateur — a sport that athletes take part in for pleasure rather than money

Christian was Kurt's first opponent in the WWF.

STARDOM

Kurt quickly rose to fame in WWE. He called himself the All-American Hero and bragged about his victories. Kurt told the audience he had achieved them by using the "Three I's" – intensity, integrity, and intelligence. Most fans disliked Kurt because he acted like he was smarter and stronger than other wrestlers.

Kurt's second TV appearance was filmed in his hometown of Pittsburgh. Kurt came into the ring wearing 21 medals to show off how great he was. He was supposed to be a hometown hero, but the fans booed him. This reaction made Kurt happy. It meant he was playing the role of a heel very well.

In his third month of pro wrestling, Kurt won both the European and the Intercontinental belts. Then he turned his attention to the World Heavyweight title. In 2000, he won this title by beating The Rock at No Mercy. From that point on, Kurt was a WWE star.

heel — a wrestler who acts as a villain in the ring

Kurt quickly became a popular heel in WWE.

Kurt has won several TNA championship belts.

RAINING GOLD

In 2001, Kurt won the WWF Hardcore Championship. He also captured the WCW World Heavyweight, the WWF Heavyweight, and the WCW United States titles. He also joined The Alliance. The Alliance was a group of wrestlers from World Championship Wrestling (WCW) and Extreme Championship Wrestling (ECW). The Alliance wanted to take over pro wrestling. But Kurt was really a spy for the WWF. In the final match at Survivor Series 2002, he helped the WWF win against the Alliance. And he wasn't shy about taking all the credit for the win.

But sometimes Kurt's pride got him in trouble. He challenged Edge to a Hair versus Hair match in 2002. Whoever lost would have his head shaved. When Edge won, Kurt tried to run away. But Edge caught him and dragged him to the barber's chair.

Even without his hair, Kurt was a champ. But WWE requires a demanding schedule. Eventually, Kurt wanted out. In August 2006, he was released from his WWE contract. Kurt planned to rest for a while. Then he surprised everyone by joining TNA wrestling just a short time later.

Chapter 4

KURT'S TIME IN TNA

At Genesis 2006, Kurt was determined to break Samoa Joe's winning streak. Kurt was locked in a tough battle. He tried to fight back but wasn't having much luck. Even giving Samoa Joe two *German suplexes* in a row wasn't enough.

Samoa Joe hit Kurt with his knee. Then he lifted Kurt on his shoulders and dropped him. This move usually finished his opponents. But somehow Kurt broke the pin and kept fighting. He slammed Samoa Joe and put him in an ankle lock. Samoa Joe kicked Kurt off and charged. Kurt moved just in time, and Samoa Joe hit his shoulder on the ring post. Kurt reapplied the ankle lock. Samoa Joe reached for the ropes to break the hold, but he couldn't make it. The hold was too painful, and Samoa Joe tapped out. Kurt had broken Samoa Joe's winning streak.

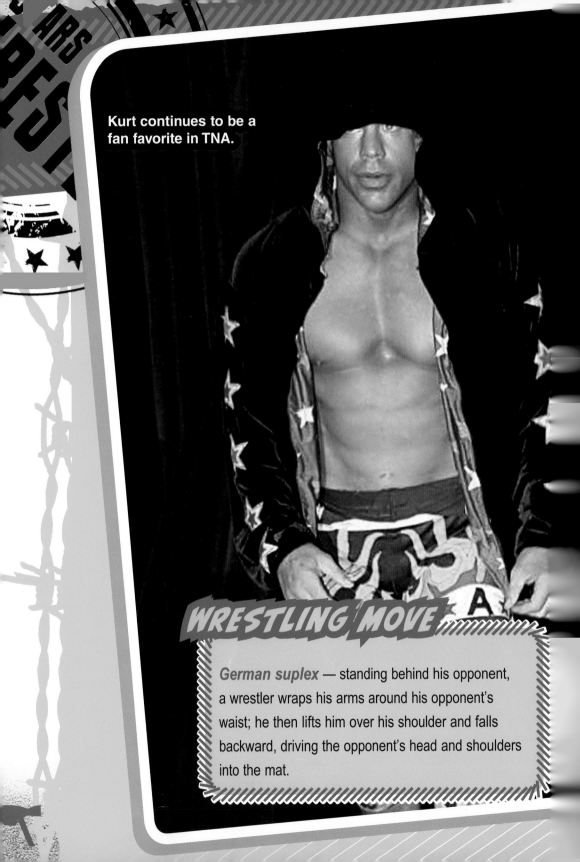

Kurt continues to be a
fan favorite in TNA.

WRESTLING MOVE

German suplex — standing behind his opponent,
a wrestler wraps his arms around his opponent's
waist; he then lifts him over his shoulder and falls
backward, driving the opponent's head and shoulders
into the mat.

TNA World Heavyweight Champion

During the King of the Mountain match at Slammiversary 2007, Kurt faced Samoa Joe again. This time Kurt also had to wrestle Christian Cage, A. J. Styles, and Chris Harris.

In 2005, Kurt won his WrestleMania match against Shawn Michaels.

All five men battled one another. Sometimes two men teamed up. To win the match, a wrestler needed to pin another wrestler. Then he needed to hang the belt from a cord high above the ring.

Harris held the belt and was on top of the ladder. Samoa Joe climbed the ladder to stop him, but Harris knocked him off. Then Cage climbed up but was knocked off too. Suddenly Styles climbed to the top rope. He leapt feetfirst toward the ladder and kicked it over.

After fighting off his opponents again, Harris picked up the ladder and spun it around. He knocked down Cage and Kurt. Then he started up the ladder with the belt. Cage knocked over the ladder and smacked Harris with it. This time Cage took the belt and started to climb.

Kurt finally got up, climbed the ladder, and put Cage in an ankle lock. They kept fighting until Harris jumped off the top rope and speared Kurt off the ladder. Kurt recovered and hung the belt moments later. He sat on top of the ladder and raised his hands in victory.

ALL THE GOLD

The win at Slammiversary 2007 gave Kurt his first TNA championship title. But it was not his last title. At one point he held three TNA titles at the same time. He held the Tag Team title, the World Championship title, and the X-Division title. He had now been a champion in the Olympics, WWE, and TNA.

Kurt then decided to compete for wrestling championships throughout the world. In 2007, he signed up for New Japan Pro Wrestling. He wrestled and beat Brock Lesnar for the International Wrestling Grand Prix (IWGP) Heavyweight Championship.

WHAT THE FUTURE HOLDS

Wrestling has always been a big part of Kurt's life. He has even said he'd like to teach wrestling when he retires. But that's not the only thing he wants to do.

Kurt has already written an autobiography about his life called *It's True! It's True!* He has also had some small movie roles. Whether he is wrestling, writing, or acting, there is no doubt that Kurt will prove himself a winner.

Kurt works hard to be successful outside of the wrestling ring.

GLOSSARY ★ ★ ★ ★ ★

amateur (AM-uh-chur) — a sport that athletes take part in for pleasure rather than money

autobiography (aw-tuh-by-AH-gruh-fee) — a book in which the author tells about his or her life

endurance (en-DUR-anss) — the ability to keep doing an activity for long periods of time

heel (HEEL) — a wrestler who acts as a villain in the ring

inspire (in-SPIRE) — to influence and encourage someone to do something

recruit (ri-KROOT) — to get a person to join

vertabrae (VUR-tuh-bray) — small bones that make up a backbone

READ MORE ★ ★ ★ ★ ★ ★

Price, Sean Stewart. *Chris Jericho.* Stars of Pro Wrestlers. Mankato, Minn.: Capstone Press, 2010.

Shields, Brian, and Kevin Sullivan. *WWE Encyclopedia.* New York: DK Publishing, 2009.

★ ★ INTERNET SITES

FactHound offers a safe, fun way to find Internet sites related to this book. All of the sites on FactHound have been researched by our staff.

Here's all you do:

Visit *www.facthound.com*

FactHound will fetch the best sites for you!

INDEX ★ ★ ★ ★ ★ ★ ★

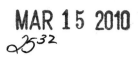

W9-AEX-843